W9-AUN-987

SWANS

designed and written by Althea
illustrated by Joe Blossom

Longman Group USA Inc.

Published in the United States of America by Longman Group USA Inc.
© 1985, 1988 Althea Braithwaite

Originally published in Great Britain in a slightly altered form by Longman Group UK Limited

ISBN: 0-88462-194-4   (library bound)
ISBN: 0-88462-195-2   (paperback)

Printed in the United States of America

88 89 90 10 9 8 7 6 5 4 3 2 1

Library of Congress Cataloging-in-Publication Data

Althea.
  Swans.

  (Life-cycle books / Althea)
  Summary: Describes the appearance, habits, migration, reproduction, and family life of this beautiful, large bird.
  1. Mute swan--Juvenile literature. [1. Swans] I. Blossom, Joe, ill. II. Title. III. Series: Althea. Life-cycle books.
  QL696.A52A47   1988   598.4'1   88-13856
  ISBN 0-88462-194-4
  ISBN 0-88462-195-2 (pbk.)

Notes for parents and teachers
Life-Cycle Books have been specially written and designed as a simple, yet informative, series of factual nature books for young children.

The illustrations are bright and clear, and children can "read" the pictures while the story is read to them.

The text has been specially set in large type to make it easy for children to follow along or even to read for themselves.

Swans are beautiful big birds.
Some live in city parks,
and some are wild.
Not all swans are alike.
Mute swans cannot make loud noises.
They grunt and hiss when angry
or frightened and use a special
yelping call for their young.

4

The swans bend their
long necks to feed
on plants that grow
in the water.

They go head down,
tail up to find food
and the small stones
that help them digest
what they eat.

Two young swans,
male and female,
attract each other
by showing off.
They arch their necks and turn
their heads from side to side.
They dip their heads in the water.

These two swans may live
together as a pair for
a year before they mate.

Mute swans do not mate until
they are three or four years old.
A pair of birds may stay together
for as long as they live.

They choose a safe place,
then the female builds the nest.
The male passes her pieces of
reed to help with the work.
He chases away other swans
that swim too near.

The female lines the nest with
pieces of plants and some of
her own soft feathers.
Next she stamps her feet and
rocks her body from side to side
to make a comfortable bowl shape.

She lays an egg every two days
until she has six or so.
Then she sits on the eggs to keep
them warm until it is time for
the eggs to hatch.

12

The male sometimes guards
the nest at night while his mate
goes off for a quick meal.
After five weeks, the eggs hatch.

The swan chicks stay
snuggled up to their mother
for a few days before
being taken on the water.

When the family goes swimming
both the parent birds keep a
close watch on their young.

The big swans are white, but
their chicks are gray.
The little ones soon pick up
food for themselves, but
their parents reach deep down
to pull up leafy plants for them.

When they are tired
the baby swans climb up
on their mother's back.
They nestle between her wings
while she goes on eating.

At night the swans return to
the nest to sleep. The chicks snuggle
under their mother's warm feathers.

A swan's short legs
and huge webbed feet
make it look clumsy
when it walks on land.

In the water, a swan can
swim very fast. It changes
direction by using its legs
to turn itself about.

When not in a hurry,
a swan may rest one leg.
First it dries its foot
in the sun, then it tucks
the foot under its wing.

Swans are among the heaviest
flying birds. They must always
take off and land on water.
They run along the water flapping
their wings to get airborne.

Little swans can learn to fly when
they are four months old and
sometimes the family all flies together.

Some swans live where winters are very cold. They fly south to find a warmer place to stay.

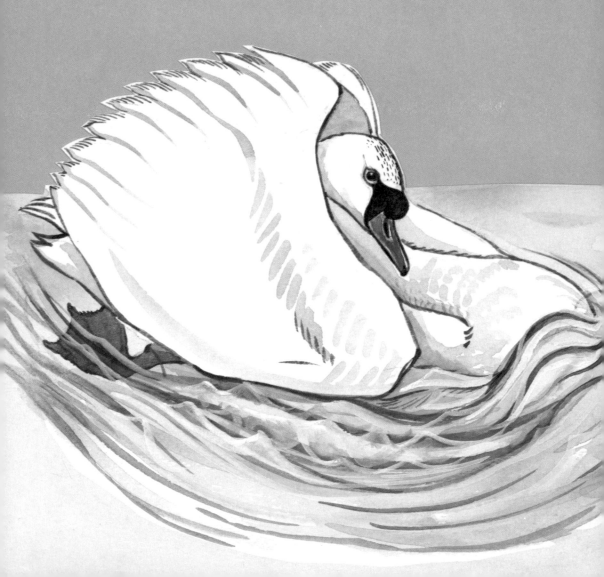

By spring, the young swans'
gray feathers are changing into white,
but their beaks are still pink.

The young birds, almost grown-up,
are chased off by their parents.
They join groups of other
young swans.

24

The parent birds can now start to get their nest ready for a new family.

SWANS, geese and ducks belong to the same bird family. They have in common flat beaks, short legs, webbed feet, short tails and long necks. All are at home on the water. They use their beaks to smooth and oil their feathers to keep them waterproof.

Of the seven kinds of swans, the mute is pictured here. These swans, originally European, were introduced in North America as decorative birds, seen in parks, for example. Some, however, have become wild. Two native swans are the trumpeter and the whistling swans, named for their cries.

All swans are powerful flyers, some with a wing span of six feet and speed of forty or more miles an hour. They usually build nests near the water, sometimes on small islands. Eggs hatch in 28 to 32 days, somewhat longer for the mute.

Young swans, called cygnets, unlike many baby birds, hatch with bodies protected by a warm coat of soft gray down. They are surprisingly independent and soon feed themselves on insects and small crustaceans, although as adults they are usually vegetarians.

Mute swans differ from other swans in the curve of their necks, the black knob on their foreheads, and their bright orange beaks. As she swims, a mother mute swan lets her babies shelter under her feathers, safe from cold and enemies.

Although wild swans have few natural predators, they have been killed by hunters and disease. Once listed in the United States as an endangered species, the trumpeter swan now appears to have escaped extinction and has indeed enlarged its breeding area.